T0114655

Woven Notions

Kenya McGhee

authorHOUSE®

AuthorHouse™
1663 Liberty Drive
Bloomington, IN 47403
www.authorhouse.com
Phone: 833-262-8899

Published by AuthorHouse 03/29/2023

ISBN: 979-8-8230-0495-4 (sc)
ISBN: 979-8-8230-0494-7 (e)

Library of Congress Control Number: 2023906038

Print information available on the last page.

Any people depicted in stock imagery provided by Getty Images are models, and such images are being used for illustrative purposes only.
Certain stock imagery © Getty Images.

This book is printed on acid-free paper.

Preface

A pure innocent seed that has been through an unfathomable journey in her life at birth she was dropped in disruptive toxic contaminated soil to thrive staying alive she cultivated toxic damaged fruit.

She currently has been uprooted and replanted in a more nourishing wholesome soil where she's arisen germinating her flows from a fresh pleasant bountiful harvest with countless revisions.

-Author

"The Shedding of our Skin"

I am writing about the transition from lost now found
Darkness to light, one being into another, death to life
Old skin to new skin
Its like the rejuvenation of skin
The restoring of flesh over flesh of an open wound
And that does not happen all at once but over a duration of time

Little by little not specific but unpredictable start to finish
My skin was tough, tough as leather
It had to be broken in sat and stomped on over time
It was mis-used an abused
Unappreciated contaminated and unpurified with uncleanliness toxic substances,
people, places and things
Mis-guided with ill desires and will
But by grace my transformation had begun
Before it was to late there was a death to life ending activated

In my darkest space in my mess
The shedding of my skin had begun
There was a shift in my ways, My desires, My walk and talk
My mind and heart had started to align up with the whispers of Gods divine word
My old skin of the one-track roads, addictions, attitudes and desires
I no longer craved or desired
My mouth was filled with affirming empowerment for myself and others
I was able to articulate the things I felt, thought, wanted and needed liked and
disliked

–Author

Speaking fluent in the moments with no more hesitation or reluctancy holding my words or fear
I am shedding my broken past of my childhood strongholds and obstacles
Letting go of my resentments and anything that has kept me in chains
Ive moved from complacency to contentment with a peace and understanding I cant explain
Compelled to be of service and good works with a drive of passion energy and love
I AM SHEDDING
No longer stagnant in my engrafted past
Now free and flying through the fog, trauma and strongholds that once hindered me and my growth in so many ways

Today my mind is renewed with thoughts and visions of life and light
My new skin enables me to persevere on in faith and hope
Trusting and dreaming of an abundant life sober and free
To properly handle and face life gratefully

Overcoming any of its obstacles that may come up against me
I am shedding with new profound revelations an abilities
My shedding has provided me with a variety of new talents and gifts
Something that my old skin would have never allowed
Continuing to shed "The Shedding of my Skin"

-Author

Contents

"FAMILY"

URBAN LYRICS

Inspiration, Motivation,

Encouragement

Changing Perspectives On The Outlook Of Life

Pace yourselves
Eat a piece of life day by day
And if thats to heavy and your a light eater
Try an hour at a time
And to all the snackers how about minute by the minute
Take a deep breath and breathe
Balance your days
Now whats on your plate

"I Wanna Be That Light"

I wanna be that light facilitating broken lost souls out of the dark night
Rescuing them from their hindering bondage
Guiding them away from this spiritual barren wasteland
Escaping the enemies carnage
Feeding their thirsty souls with essential nourishing life sustaining roads
Cleansing them with holy water
Showers of the one and only dominion and power
Leverage and coverage over every hour
Draping them in the first love of affection
Renewing their visions
As they sit in the palm of his hand of protection
Motivation, Fresh salvation
With a mindset set on a predestined heavenly location
I wanna be a light thats shouting from a mountain top about my testimonial life,
Of how he brought me out, Of how my soul was cleansed
And how he turned my sin to win
Breathing into me new life
Healed and restored by his stripes
Having the privilege to live two lives in one
Again another chance just to get it right
Beauty for ashes, Death to life, Revisionary sight
Brazen abilities to shine my light

I wanna be that light
That worship him on a purpose for a purpose
Surrendering my own self-will
Glorifying and praising him, Hallelujah, Thank you Jesus
Holy spirit filled
Discerning that these tangible emotions are real, Sending me chills

Let me be that light
Never would of made it if I didnt choose to follow his will and take this flight
Ascending me up to heightened heights
Content and peacefully soaring so high
Over any afflictions, Conqueroring my obstructing addictions
My armour, shield, and sword
Sending the angels before me on the battlefield

So any contention that strikes I can calmly ignore
Making me one with you
Conducively collaborating our lights
To allieviate this secular strife
I wanna be that light

"A Quilt"

A quilt an abstract piece of art
Uniquely decorated woven together layers of cloth
Full of designs
Heavy weighted some light subtle and fine
A diverse state of mind
Independently one of a kind

Comfortable and soft
In some seasons Im lost
Colorful noticeable, Laid upon adoreable
Slept with at times my conditions had become deplorable
Padded replicated patterns past down through our lineage
A history cut up and threaded
Worn out, torn and ripped

Every distinctive segment narrates a story from gory to glory
The trials and strongholds that has been afflicted and hitched
Trimmed on salvaged intricately gathered fabric
Thats been well kept loosened then stitched
Repaired, protected, flexible and stretched
Put to the enemies test

Reinvented, Refurbished Death to life, Calvary
As of now its condition is at its best
Inestimable sentimental value, Priceless nothing less
Covering the soul
Comforting the confused, frightened, worried and cold
Filling of feathers for the wholesomely well wings
To fly away from the stains of the faded colors of dye
When temptation attempted to damage and pry
The smell is southern old and stale from the enduring rain from life lapsed storms
Nevertheless it drapes me with warm fuzzies
No pain its loving
Stiff my quilt is so comforting
And fuzzy its lovely
A Quilt

"They Dont Know"

They dont know what you have done
They dont know what your word transforms
They dont know the joy, comfort an inner enlightenment you bring Faith
They cant feel the untangible or even see the unseen
They dont understand the lyrics from my heart of the songs that I sing

They dont know, They dont know
Until they weather their storms an escape this earthly harm
Touching the hem of your garment is what sounded my alarm

They dont understand that your my helmet, sword and shield
They cant discern the goosebumps that I receive from your assurance and confirmation thrills
Or either take into account the blood that was spilled for our sin
That restore and heals

They dont know

They dont know that my worship is for real
They dont understand how my indescribable peace remains so still
Or how imperative it is for me to feed off of your daily bread in attempts to dodge the enemy temptations and follow your will

They cant see how you assisted me to conquer my strongholds and triumph over the enemy
Unsealing my blinded vision
Whispering in my ear that you are one of my own and as of today you are living
They dont know how your life sustaining nourishment fullfills

Breathing into me new life
Power alleiviating my strife
A new creation
Providing within me a greater substance
That instills a brighter purpose for my life
They dont know but I can never unknow

"Its Given"

Its given living life intentional I awake daily in attunement living life on a purpose for a purpose
Germinating my flow
My ambition is struggle driven
My strengths derived from resiliency is flamboyantly noticeable its given
Im colorful so if you dont understand me its because we are all singly uniquely woven
Our reasoning may appear diverse its due to the separate lives were living but its given

That you are you and I am me

Comfortably positioned as what our creator and character has defined us to be
With inevitable cultural engraving
Ancestral imprints of enslavement oppression pavements
Its given resiliency
You are you and I am me
Fearlessly and wonderfully made to stand as one in unity and love through these perilous times
So I shine my light and humanize life by vocalizing

My voice towards a more positive wholesome choice
Combating against the enemies hate and loud overwhelming noise
A beacon of light to penetrate, motivate and inspire those that can relate
Breaking lost souls free from bondage
At one point I was captive hidden in silence

I subjugated the trauma and prioritized my hurt
Sifting through my dirt I dug up my worth
No more comparing today Im comfortable in my own skin
No matter my failures or imperfections
The reflection in the mirror positively affirm that I can win

Revelations to articulately convey the words to heal
What is given that you are you and I am me
Walking down the same road with dissimilar backgrounds

But independently we can stand on common ground understanding one another in love
Not letting the curve of division subdue neither the stench of contention to pursue
Eroding the plans that were set for our creation
Our connections will birth greater revelations

So lets live life intentional in unification
With more worldwide harmonious peaceful relations
Its given that you are you and I am me
Distinguishably in acceptance of who we all were woven to be
It is Given

"All Purpose Woman"

A jack of all trades
She has the patient of an animal in the wild waiting to devour its prey
Spiritually driven she attends worship every Sunday she stay on her knees in prayer
And when the impossible occur her superhumanly powers make the impossible possible in the most effortless calmest way
An all purpose woman that surpasses any limit day after day

When the pressure of life events weighs on her soul
Uprooted strengths appear out of the dirt and she persevere on not letting the issues take its toll
In her dreams she can interpret her deposited notions
And without any obstructing negative doubts she reach for her goals
Exposing her thoughts putting her visions into motion

An all purpose woman who prioritize
Because she is the prize
Passionate and understanding with no judgements about any situation she encounter
Jumping into other people shoes to experience their walk Enlightening
She talks articulating her emotions and thoughts

She will listen, Full of ambition, Self-sufficient
Getting dirty taking the trash out wont interrupt her mission
Shes a scholar and its not to many things that will bother her Performances of a mother and a father

She will work cook and clean
Versatile so masculine duties are never a thing
And when things are invisible her sight can see the unseen
Shes brilliant, An innovator
Never wore the label of a hater

Free from toxic contaminates sober and clean
No matter the stormy weather a joyous smile will remain on her face and still be seen
Standing firm on her faith it could never be replaced
Attitude is never dampened shes never mean

She has a beautiful amazing spirit
And is considered a great support team

Sweet as candy, Forevermore green
Free as the soaring white dove
All purpose, On a purpose for a purpose
She shines her light uplifting, Empowering attracting others toward the spotlight
Shes that all purpose woman thats magnificently out of sight

"I Walk This Way For A Reason"

I walk this way for a reason
For all the unfathomable weight Ive carried throughout every season
For all the multiplied calculated pain after doing my math
For every broken lost soul that Ive encountered crossing my path

For my former days of trash
For my victorious testimonial past
For the treasures Ive salvaged through the hurt of my dirt
For my life lesson discoveries
Realizing in my latter days that it was Jesus blood that protected and covered me

Releasing what the enemy exposed
Facilitating me to overcome my heavy weighted anchored strongholds
Never putting to much on me that I cant bare
Im discerning that your presence has always been here

I walk this way from the muscles Ive cultivated
Resilient, Fortitude driven when the trauma was penetrated
Pushing through the dark spaces that encompassed me
Or what about when the enemy had me hooked
Corrupted, Burnt and cooked
My darkest deepest moments I fell into the prison system
Im shook

Isolated stuck
My eyes and ears are opened
Im listening, Im up

Now understanding that my Higher power was waiting for me to return to his
open arms to deliver me
His word is my strength
Salvation is what he instilled in me

Im walking this way to be a light
That I can model, Guide and shift perspectives
And extract out a fresh positive awakened life
To renew your hope

Broaden your faith scope
An advise you to adhere to what the prophets wrote
To allieviate your walk
By abiding and believing what the living written word has taught

Im walking this way for so many countless reasons
Devoted strides throughout all of my present and future seasons

"The Beacon"

Signaling all the broken lost souls to recovery the beacon of light illuminated the community
Propelling them to new levels
Inspirationally guiding them away from carnal attractions
Unsealing their visions to greater perspectives oppose to this mundane living
She was providing spiritual healing
Through the living written word of God

Delivered, Converted she conformed to his will
The Holy spirit was instilled it gave her chills

Provision draped her character
Fresh salvation rearranged a new narrator in her life
She planted seeds from the fruits of her spirit
And when God sent the rain it germinated its harvest
Once revealed the broken lost souls had started to feel it

After recognizing the developments they were able to withstand and triumph over the enemies battlefield of strongarmed events
No longer bound and in its hand
Fully equip their lamps had been lit
Conducingly collaborating with the beacon to permeate the universe
Exhibiting a greater purpose and worth they conjoined their lights
Join the light to facilitate in conquering this worldly fight

"Rich Why You Broke"

Im rich while Im broke
Yes that what I stated and its not a humorous joke
Im rich with the jewels of my tools
Thats been produced in the sporadic turbulence rain of my storms
Standing in contentment with no complaints Im rich

Im rich in influence
A light to the broken lost souls thats trying to escape the treacherous night
Harriet Tubman sights
Leading souls out of bondage to freedom with visions and actions of instilled
determination persevering towards whatever Im pursuing
Im rich

No matter the obstacle big or small
Uncomfortable with fears
Courageously Ill attempt to conquer it letting my faith steer

Rich in this profound new light
Awakened
Risen out of my grave a new creation
A fresh life to generate power
Leverage and coverage over every hour
Praises to the one and only dominion and power
Rich

Rich in the filthy muddy soil of my darkest fallen pits
Im still rich
Understanding that you have to get dirty in order to experience this lift

Rich in the fruits of the spirit
Blessed to be afflicted
Holy spirit filled
Convicted
Thanking God that I can discern and hear it

Im rich while Im broke and its not a humorous joke
Im rich

"Im A Strong Black Woman"

Im a strong black woman that has sojourned through many storms
Wearing a facade of many faces
That were not of my usual norm

A Mother and a Father figure of five
Are the acquired skills that I have performed

Carrying the pressures of unfathomable weight
Layers of my skin had to be shed before I arrived to this awakened robust state
The stripes inflicted across my back are scars considered as my badges of honor
And if you look closely reading between the lines it will tell you the personal
stories of my travel
Throughout my life era of trauma

When my world had shifted after the judge striked his gavel
When controled substances invaded my being
And my self-discipline began to unravel
When consoling unhealthy relations pursued
And my self-esteem was dismantled

Today Ive overcame my distant walks of all those rocky roads
The blisters and calluses on my feet are healed
While the token of undefeated is freely flowing through my soul

Bruises and blemishes, Reminders of the traumatic pain
Are only indicators of my superhumanly resilient gain
Attaining the life sustaining discoveries
Through my lessoned experience strain

Ima strong black woman
That's fully assembled from her restored collected ruins
Flourishing put together remains

My life is a testimony
So today I can proudly stand in my stance
Flamboyantly stating my prison number and name
As the imperfect strong black woman that I am
Ima strong black woman

"Fear"

Intimidating obstructing insecurities
Planting seeds of inadequacy
Fear in the mind
Hindering and paralyzing our goals
Questioning ourselves do we qualify am I good enough to take on any upper level
roads

Trauma taunting fear that steers the mental
Hiding and isolating your gifts restraining your voice
Against the world its makes the perception of you feel little
Will my accomplishments be recognized or merit based
Will they relate can I reach that upper level place
Or will I continue to live invisible, Hidden, Mis-placed

Will I be respected or will my race be in vain
After enduring all the storms of life pain
Can I let my vision and spirit reign
Liberating this loaded locked up strain

Even when Im rejected I still manage to maintain
Articulating my emotions against the rain to the grain

Decompressing scribing my feeling and thoughts on this paper
In order to release my consolidated lyrical vapors
Like a baby chick bursting out of its shell
I escape breaking loose from the fear
Flying free over my obstacles crying elation tears
The spotlight is now on my journey even though it had took me several years
To expose and discover my true identity and triumph over my fears
As of today I am here standing with no fears

"The Gift Is Me"

The gift is my renewed mindset instilling in me immense fortitude
To overcome any overwhelming events
Allowing me not to conform to this temporal prison community norm
And to continue to let my higher power develop my form

The gift is my resiliency drawn from my supernatural roots
Providing me my truths
Assisting me to stand and boldly walk along my journey
As I bounce back and shed my skin into the new

The gift is the privilege to walk in this refined creation
Having the advantage of once again another chance
To enjoy the rest of my life with my love ones
Repositioning my character defects towards a different stance

The gift is my innovating manic mental ability of a serial hustle
A jack of all trades flipping checks to get paid
An inherited hustle
With a freshly birthed more positive tussle
Presently embarking on a more legitimate muscle

The gift is my reflection of my shine illuminating the universe
While residing in my ordained allotted time
Transcending above any negative restraints to grind
Jumping out on any productive avenue of revenue to reach out and grab whats
mine

The gift is me

This beautiful woven creation that God has shaped and molded me to be
Despite my failures or past calamities
The gift is simply me.....

"Escaped Identity"

She was just an ordinary girl
Who liked to introvert inside her own little world
Introspecting her very own unique being
Getting acquainted with the reflection of the strangers face in the mirror that she
is finally facing and seeing

During her journey she use to mimick others deliverance and appearance
Following their walk and talk
Admiring the way that they were living
Insecure not in tune with self
Envyingly lusting over other peoples wealth

Consumed with fear she wanted to be accepted
And never have to experience the emotions of abandonment
Or either be neglected, Rejected
In avoidance she shielded her reflections
Not wanting to see her authentic self
Incapable of handling reality

She placed her visions and goals to the side up on the shelf
Dreaming of being perfected
Not knowing or visually seeing who christ created her to be
She was sleep going through the hurdles in life
Until she fell on her face surrendering praying on her knees
Then her faith and vision resurfaced in her darkest space
Introduced with the woman as of now she can accept and face

Dispelling the consumed feeling of feebleness and dismay
Shes no longer abiding by these fleshly driven laws
Trying to fit in with a specific crowd
Or worried about her weight big in size or small
Hated or uneducated being accepted by others

She escaped all the unhealthy corruption
When insecurities an inadequacy conveyed its mental health and sabotaging
self-medicated addictions
Not understanding the extent of what was placed on her plate

Society couldnt relate
To the tormenting dual diagnosis that was related
When your on the battlefield combating mental health
Without the proper help

That explains the unfortunate suicide as part of an escape
She escaped
She had a moment to pause and recognize Gods faith
Started applying Gods perspective daily to navigate
Through her days
Reflecting on her past walk of how he kept her in good condition
After venturing off into that wilderness of desperation
Out so far away
Lost now found

She learned to embrace her imperfections
Growing impervious to her flaws
No matter the cause her head is held high holding its replaced crown
Blessed with the fruits of the spirit standing tall

Re-adjusting her focus on what really matters
Her elevated self-esteem has assisted her to climb up the ladder out of her secluded
space
Breaking free from her confined restricted limitation zone
Uncomfortably complacent

Courageously exploring new destinations
Oppose to her unhealthy comfortable zone
Her incubated safe space
Where she was living life in the darkness
Perceiving that she was safe
Not really experiencing the true enjoyment of her unique life race
Out of place
But as of now she escaped

"Focus"

My GPS is rerouting me from where my intended locations were set
Ive called off all bets
Letting the Holy spirit guide me towards whats best
Nevertheless
I focus driving forward shedding my spotlight

Focused collaborating with other bright lights
I understand its hard to bypass this illuminating light
My intentional purpose is to brightly shine uplift and direct
With imprints of empowerment
Not to deliberately blind and distract your sight
Or niether be maliciously attacked due to my light by evil spite

Im uniquely woven, A revised citizen, An additive to the chosens
Wholesomely equip to convey my past fails
Formulating my testimonial concepts into victorious tales
Revealing how I overcame my strongholds of the enemy spells

Focus not on me but my focus
Maybe then you would make that uncomfortable shift and re-focus your focus
Superhuman with extraordinary powers
Leverage and coverage over every hour

Dressed with the stares because I am extraordinaire
Unaccustomed to the usual
I self-direct so please dont interject
Loved, My positive vibes reflect

With a mindset of my own
So my focus is not driven by what you think I should do
I focus on only what my purpose has driven me to do
So please dont hate it
You cant do nothing but respect it or congratulate it
Im focused
The gain is to focus not on me but my focus
Re-focus your focus and maybe then you'll focus

"Doing What I Do"

Believing in myself I just keep doing what I do
Innovating my craft, Protecting my anointing
Steering clear from shady substances
People places and things that seems to bring on issues

Uplifting, positivity, Motivational are my best lanes to choose
Surrounding myself around gossip and drama under the weather feeling blue
Now thats not what I like to do
Im just doing what I do
Reaching new horizons stepping out of my favorite shoes
With a renewed mindset thats robustly built and could never lose

With no procrastination up against this time Ima dive in
The race of life swimming boldly upstream striving for my place
Out of my dark normal comfortable space
With no delay doing what I do

Its never an easy task wearing this self-discipline mask
Your will power will be tested daily
While temptations will occur persuading
You to falter and disregard your evolution
Awakening your surrendered past disruptive pollution

That you have relinquished and laid to rest
Resurfacing the corrupting paved paths that you onced walked through to live
life today at your best
Ima just keep doing what I do
Not concerned about anyone or anything else
Just keeping the focus on my moves
Doing what I do
Living life at its best

"He Patiently Awaits"

Jumping into the undefeated streets the traffic was moving fast
Addictive corruption was speeding outta control
Uncertain of how I survived or how my existence even last
The enemy was on a mission
The Holy spirit was contributing to my intuition
Ill emotions, Feel'n bad I didnt listen
Currency driven, Luxurious livin is what I was fish'n
In the water neck deep
Inundated waters growing obstructing my speech
Trying to keep my head afloat I can hardly breathe
The pressure had become so overwhelming that it completely knocked me off my feet
Drowned, was lost now found
I had risen from out of the grave and now back walking on ground
Resuscitated, breathed into me new life
Relinquishing my old will and sight
Currently walking with a new identity in new light
Healed and restored by his stripes
Grateful for his mercy and patient
I was totally surprise with open arms he was still welcomely awaiting
Just for Lil lost me to come back around
He calmly whispered God Bless you my child your now safe and sound

"A Jailbird Cry"

Have you ever heard a jailbird cry
Its outer body is alive but its inner soul has died
In several attempts it try to resuscitate its life
It tries and tries

But its heartbeat is faint and it no longer thrives to stay alive
Agony is dressed all over its face
Life had been misplaced by its human mistakes
Mental notions of wishing to retrace those past dates
But its way to late

So the jailbird simmer in the heat of what has been placed on its plate
Most just like to debate
But there is a few that can relate of how it got caged inside those gates
There is no sweet sound only frowns crying out sorrow
Pushing through the calendar days in hopes of a brighter tomorrow
Swallowing its grief to combat the undefeat of confinement
Digesting all of its wrongs
Never crying the jailbird hums
Its liberating jailbird song

Have you ever heard a jailbird cry
It tries and tries but its soul just wont abide

"Making Amends"

Making amends
The reconciliation of old friends
When disharmony arose and the once so solid frozen ice was thin
The conflict broke it and we all had fell in
Without genuine forgiveness the division is sin
Now how can we move foward and win

With added pressure weighing us down
Voids from the past connected companionships that were once so amicably sound
Lets demonstrate greatness
Lets communicate about our issues
Apologize then put it to rest

Lets forgive and forget
Life is to short to be at one anothers neck
Its all about maturity, Loyalty and respect
So lets reunite and move on to whats next

Whether we agree to disagree
In love we all got to do whats best
Prevailing over the enemies test

Making amends with old friends
Theres no need to say anything else
Make Amends

"A Dream"

I had a dream that things were'nt as bad as it really seemed
I had triumphed over all my enslaved habits from my past upbringing
My new life was green
With fresher scenes
No disruptive substances dwelled in any person, place or thing
No more oppression
Love was lethal
So we never had to worry about any negative sequels
Everyone was equal

United every nationality and religion
No division
Similar to Martin Luther King there was a vision
I had a dream that united we stood together as a team
Compassion was prevalent
Heavy worldwide
The noxious hate was lean
I had a dream
But after I opened my eyes I realized that it wasnt reality
Not what it had seemed it was only a dream
My dream
I had a dream

"I must go on"

I must go on
Dragging my broken soul through these penetrating storms
Bent over fallen to my knees
Humanizing my restraint voice
Liberating my internal hurt
Im steady moving on
Humming my freedom song
My palms and knees are scraping the ground
Asking God please

Provide me with strength and deliver me
From all of my iniquities
Alleviate the weight and pressure thats continuously being afflicted upon me

Im sliding further in the shedded blood of my created chaos
My self inflicted wounds and scrapes
Thanking God for the blood that heals and drapes
My body
Covering me from head to toe

In assurance these wounds will heal and everything I loss will soon be restored
tenfold
Persevering on through I am closer than close
Noticing the light
Thats captivating my sight
Opening my eyes instilling provision

Relieved
Now a lighter load is driven
Drawing me towards a greater stand on faith
As the Holy Spirit enlightens
The storms diminishes

With fortitude Im back standing even stronger
With abilities to administer what has been revealed and so freely given to me
A walking testimony
I am going on

"Self-Care"

Extraordinaire
Beware of my self-care
They stare but who cares
Im blunt, Straight to the point, Know what I want
Dont have to front, Confident, Bold
No longer outta control
Flaunting my valuable victorious junk

Beautifully selfish
Recognizing my worth feeling wealthyish
Unnoticeable at birth I was blind
But now I can understand and see myself in the mirror
Not easily affected by the chitter chatter secular realm
The loud noise that dont even matter
My ears are opened to relevance
I demonstrate rigorous poise amongst the noise
No penetration from the chitter chatter

Rocking these worn out soles
I have traveled many miles
Many roads and still manage to smile
And when the animal of the storms attack
Instilled with the Holy spirit I carry the cross on my back
Never settling in lack
Persistent pedalling You will then hear me growl
Conqueror warrior style

An overcomer of trials over trials
A testimonial child
Very gentle loving and calm
I dont need to get loud
So beware because I self-care
Liberating my soul
More precious than finest quality of any gold
Even when I grow old
Ill still be representing my best mold
Self-care

"Goals"

Goals are chosen roads leading to our accomplishments
They can be big or small
Working towards them gradually brings elevation to all

Setting them provides us purpose
Instilling worth in us
Leading us to believe as our action proceeds
We will then achieve
And successful progression will visually be seen

Alleviating our strife
And instantaneously produce in us a revived life

"Reset"

Thinking ahead in another time zone
Deposits of mental notes are being applied to my dome
Throughout all of this time I been stepping in stride
Cultivating my strengths
Preparation of mental and physical abilities anticipating on whats next to come

Im painting an even greater picture on canvas this go round
So I figure Ill need an even larger easel when I apply my color to this old town
Enthusiastically eager to influence and explode
Everything that has been strapped locked up, Binded and held captive in my soul

My emotions thoughts, My dreams and goals
My life story thats soon to be told
Reset
Focusing recognizing the profound discoveries in my failures
Paying close attention to all my losses
Which has ultimately led me to the direction of the position of becoming my own various bosses

The loss of time, success, death, failed marriage
I was stagnant stuck in my mess
Pressed by the enemies test
The loss of my parenting
The abandonment of my five children not to mention the rest
Reset letting this be my most valuable lesson
Grateful for every God given blessing

Ive reset
My vision is clear
Im vigilant an on alert with tools to cope
Holding a renewed mindset with a broader scope

I daily self-examine and routinely do checks
Learning that realistically school will always be in
Experience is life teacher it never ends

So keep an open mind for new perspectives
Actively listen to comprehend
Step out of your comfort zone trying something different to shed your old skin
to win
Demolish and rebuild and know that we all fall short
And resetting is key
Reset

"Infrastructure"

Blessed
Alive and thriving
My perseverance is driving
My strides with every step thats met
Each movement goes a long way
Accelerating the heart towards a healthier day
Combating against all ailments
In hopes to prevent any unexpected events
Consuming nourishing nutrients
Engaging in physical activity to contribute to our defense
So we exercise to extend our lives
Loosening our muscles and joints so the wont get stiff or frozen
Keeping the blood flow circulating in regular motion
Assisting the routine functions of the organs
Initiating and depositing positive mental notions
Equilibrium system
With a robust base firmly grounded as we stand in our place
Physically fit to compete as we run this life race

Im Digging Deeper

Today Im digging deeper
Getting to the root of it, Deeper
Nothing less
Not viewing or selling my self-worth cheaper
But deeper

They say the sky is the limit but I beg to differ
Because Im that drifter
And Ima boldly appear aiming to shoot past the moon
Dont feel to sit around wasting any more of my precious time with attached limitations
Captivated in bondage
Hindering affects leaving me in loom

Assuming that things will walk my way and fall into my lap
Without any reach or effort Im done with all of that
Besides my Higher power is sovereign authority over all
And anything after that
Im solely in control and responsible for in my life
And those are facts
Even when my actions are conducive to my falls

Ima dig deeper
In order to get to the root of things
The knowledge from the facts
The enlightenment of the wisdom that it brings
Deducting procrastination, Exerting all of my energy
Taking risks with no fear of the falls
Climbing every mountain whether its big or small

I gotta dig deeper
Stepping out on my faith
Something that has been so peacefully keeping me planted in contentment in my darkest space
Securing my back, Navigating my being keeping me on track
As I embark towards more enlightening revelations

Im digging deeper
Even when Im knocked off of my feet
Flat on my face
Making my way through this darkness
I feel around and there is no one else but me in this place
Feeble, No longer walking
Continual perseverance is what Im talking

With driven abilities to crawl
Crawling through my darkest loneliest valleys
Despite the stormy circumstances in all
GOD overcame the world so why should I stay stagnant in any of my falls

And when Im in my lack
Im comfortably deficient
Sitting idle with an optimistic mindset
Quiet, turning down all the noise, Self-sufficient

And in my self-awareness Im aware that this is when God steps in whispering
SHHH, Silence
I must listen

Receptive
Pure elation
Similar to God I have risen
Outta my grave with provided provision
Placing me in better positions
With uncomfortable adventurous unfamiliar ambitions

Ive dugged deeper
Ive seen the light
Accountable for all of my wrongs
And now in full acceptance of my past life
With my head held high Im no longer crawling but walking upright

Dealing and able to face my face
Face to face
The reflection thats appearing in the mirror
The phenomenal me
I can boldly stand, now back in this life race

No longer distorted or unrecognizable
Ive found a best friend
Now were better aquainted and things are much clearer
Instilled tools of preparation now were destined to win
No longer selling my soul for cheaper
Because as of today Im digging deeper
Im digging deeper

"Molds"

Broken lost souls
Never getting its chance to receive its proper mold
Cracked with defects from the initial start
Growing up with distressed suffering in the mental and heart

But once dipped in the Holy water the clay is mollified and reshaped with a greater substance
Fortified
Glazed and placed in the fire remade
Now amazed

Presented back into this world with new desires
Abundant showers of blessing
As they embark to shout and proclaim their testimonial power
Fully dressed and equip
A profound peace and a changed will is what I feel in this

A fresh start
I wont depart
Or crack this mold of this new salvation that I chose

"Flying Spirit"

Free flying beyond any limits
I love to dance and shower in the holy rain
In rememberance of my deliverance
No pain, Encouraged with no chains
Oppose to where the human spiritual slumber stand ground
Gazing up towards the sky comfortably blind on land

As I pass them by their visions are faint
They can barely see me
But have so many thoughts of wanting to be me

Mis-led they never attempt to take that step to get presented their wings to fly
An opportunity thats free of charge
To move ahead

With circles and turns I dodge temptations
As I play amongst the wind
Combating the enemy sin
Protected and peacefully out of harms way
Not worrying about any of this secular sin that blows my way

In my discernment I understand that trouble will come but wont last always
So I embrace the tormenting tingling wind that ruffle my feathers
My multicolored fruits of the heart remains flying free
As I delight in my storms or the pleasant sunny weather

My source provides
The contentment in my soul will tell no lies
And as the time elapse I will continue to fly by and by

"Shadow"

Somebody is following me
I dont know who it could be
I turned around and asked my shadow
But it just shook its head and stated its only me that you see

It never talked or taunted me
It only lived through me vicariously
Following in my paved tracks
Wanting to snatch me back when I made the wrong decisions in life and got
knocked off track

Following me all across the map
Micking my every movements
Now how amazing is that
Communicate with me a little more shadow
Help me defeat my most challenging battles

And when the light turns off resuscitate my soul
Liberating me from my creators mold

Soar among the land of the free
In the eternal world where the narrow road leads

Where the existence of demise will no longer be
But flee, were free

Inside the eternal world where no one grows old
A paradise that everyone wish to see

"Am I Good Enough"

I wasnt good enough to be your wife
But Im good enough for you to briefly stop by my house and eat off a piece of my pie
But only for a taste
Not even long enough for us to get better acquainted over an appetizing dinner
date

You say I need to keep my mouth shut dont ask questions and know my place
But my exterior was good enough for to accelerate your actions to pursue this
pie chase
Distasteful and rude
A robbery in progress with no ski mask on
You stole my jewels

Deceiving and mis-leading you had me confused
Thinking that I was the one
I just knew I was good enough for you

Am I good enough dressed with all these embedded scars and wounds from my
attacks
From the trecherous wild enemy after I drifted out into the jungle during my
past tracks
Covered inner and outer bruises and blemishes from the lacerations I sustained
in my lack

Am I good enough, Good enough for you
Am I good enough when my health starts to deteriorate leaving me ill
Medically incapacitated will you still
Stay down loyal stuck by my side on chill
Will my love and structure still satisfy and seal your heart with thrills

Will that be good enough
Understanding that sometimes over time relationships fade and situations get
rough
To tough to handle
Corrupted and dismantled

Are we good and prepared enough for that challenging rumble
Or will the valuable love of what I perceived unbreakable love that we built over
the years crumble

Am I good enough when my age is put to the test
When Im drying up gray, old and wrinkled
Looking in the mirror and my self-esteem is lowered and Im not feeling my best
Will you still see past that and see the beauty thats held within
Will we remain adhering to our vows strong holding hands
Or will you let go running in sin

"Capacity"

Expansion Im stretching myself thin
Vulnerably uncomfortable as I subject myself onto foreign roads
Naked freely flowing with the wind
Filling myself with wholesome enlightening experiences
Exploring paths that I would have never expected to choose

Courageously stepping out on faith with a concrete thought that if I keep God
first I could never lose
Going out on a limb
Taking the blindfolded risk on more positive avenues
Rearranged energy
Exerting all that street muscle
Towards a more legit hustle

Over stepping my boundaries
Surpassing any of my presumed limits
Sober, Focused in it to win it
Ignoring that hindering negative thinking
Yes I can achieve it there is no limit

Ima fill my cup till it over flow
Generous giving back what was freely given to me
Inundated success from my ambition and driven goals
Tenacious

My capacity is unknown
My dome loves to roam with a variety of flourishing concepts
I must continue to reach until I sit on my throne
There aint no time for procrastination or sleeping I can do that when Im gone
Keeping God close I cant do this alone

Fill me up and stretch me thin
My capacity is unknown
My sole purpose is to project empowerment and win
I gotta pass this light on

"Follow Me"

Follow me into a place where we can be free
Where we can flow like the waves of the sea
Distant from anything else reaching limits of the unknown
Listening to the symphony of splashes thats reciting our favorite love song
Roaming wild passing deserted islands
Settling, Building, Nestling close together in our home

Follow me under the cascades of this secular strain
Adhering to my soul
Withstanding the tormenting pain that these times unfold

Follow me when my self-worth and self-esteem is dampened
Making me feel like the finest quality of gold
Even when I grow old

Follow me up this spiritual mountain
Ascending us to greater heights
Defying all the odds
Inciting righteous strikes

Follow me, Follow me, Follow me

Even when difficult situations occur
Let me lean on you as well as you on me
When were dropped in the pot of hot boiling water
And confusion begins to stir

Follow me through my illness
My weakest moments
When Im feeling like I cant kill this
Kiss me, Comfort me, Hold me
Tell me you can heal this
Support my immune system making me feel the thrillest

Galvanize my goals putting them in motion
Accelerating all of my formulated notions
Deposited talents into the chosen
That the resurrected gifts has arose in
Follow me

"My Temporary Abode"

My temporary abode was my darkest hole.
Till the light broke through the bricks illuminating my soul,
Brighter than any gold.

Exhaustion had began to devour me while I was running through this prison time.
Then the angels appeared lifting me up assuring me that I'll be just fine.
Resuscitating my life, saving me from my despair.
Whispering in my ear, child please know that I have never left you alone.
I've always been there.

My thoughts and weaknesses were screaming enough is enough.
But God said when I am weak, I am strong.
So let the rough cultivate the tough.

Now I'm fortified full of vitality standing tall.
Overcoming it all.
Although my body still sits behind these steele gates.
My mindset and soul is free flying over these prison walls.

"My Poems Are Poetically Me"

"Family"

"Bloodline"

My DNA is a hot shot
An infected bloodline
Thats incapable of being stopped
Its contagious
Contaminating generation after generation
Addicted to the hustle grind

Best believe it, We gotta get it
And if its anything about currency increase
Were gonna see it

And over time the grind evolved
The majority of us became criminally injustice inclined
And throughout the era of our lives we served prison time

A repeated dysfunctional cycle
Now realizing that we were all out of our minds
Aware of our right and wrongs
Even though it was our regular norm

Thats the insanity of it all
We will observe and experience the put downs
Jump back up, Dust ourselves off
Then right back at it after we fall

The rush of the street life got us sprung
Gangsta life style toting guns
The risk of the fast life had strapped a rope around our necks
Suicidal style, Had us hung

Playing on a mega slide leading us down a slippery slope to our darkest pits
And when the authorities hit
We found ourselves sitting inside our created chaos
Asking why me
Digging up our roots
Reflecting wondering why we even thought it was cool to chose this shit

Hitting licks
For that easy not worth the time crime fix
Not taking heed to all the trauma and drama
The dominoe affect of the necks it would slit

Generational incisions
Repeated dysfunction is what we were breeding
Living
Giving and passing down to our innocent seeds
The unshaped children of our bloodline productions
That will eventually began to suffer and be filled with a multitude of their own voids and needs

From the negative repeated installments of the exposed actions and footsteps we were paving

Reserved destinations
Caught up in the penal system slaving
Bloodline we need to rectify this pattern and come up with a resolution
Saving our future
Providing our next generation with a more brighter safe haven

"Generations"

The filthy smell lingered generation after generation as she dipped her hands in
the multicolored paints of abuse

Raised with out not many instructed installments throughout her her own life
she was deficient in her parenting tools
The unhealthy relationships of men that she choosed
Uncertain of what roads to pursue
She held on to the only noxious love she knew

On canvas she painted a story of a women with a dual diagnosis of mental health
and drug abuse issues
And when the corrupting corroding dysfunction broke loose in her home
She carried on like normal activities
Enduring the turmoil with a sour taste in her mouth
She reflected it back onto her encountered mates, lovers, friends and innocent
seeds
Similar and familiar of what normalcy was use to
A projection of her neglected needs

She conceived and birthed her own tangible truths
Obliviously she began orchestrating another generational recycled song
Administered debilitating injections to her youths
From parents wrongs
She couldnt recognize the harm
Of the retroactive trauma being overspilled, resurfaced, and formed

Afflicted eternal brewing lacerated wounds
Periodically appearing in a fresh family unit home

The loss of her familyhood she was fearing
Distractive, overwhelming relations she was dealing
Drug abuse dominated
Paralysesus of the emotional soul had her feeling elated
Elevated perilous dysfunction she dated

As the euphoric toxins numbed the body, permeating its mold
Not removing what was engraved from her arrested developemental days
Her damaged emotions and time had only froze

As the time elapsed further on the circumstances turned grave
Only too recite the rehearsed recycled generational song of wrongs

That will replay on repeat over and over dwelling in the minds of her children
That will soon engulf their homes
Now its in rotation
Generation after generation
I wonder why no one ever focused on salvation
Recycled negativity outta control
With newfangled revelations
Evolved and unfold

"Looking For You"

Im looking for you
The super hero I idolized
Under my roof
Growing up as a child

Any male toting a gun
Slang'n narcotics, Hood
Evading authorities on the run

Street life for the majority
Easy living, Fast money
Hustling was the priority

Im looking for you in the zoo
A wild untamed animal
That seemingly my mother couldnt handle
Having her mental wires intertwined and scrambled
Adhering to her vows like super glue
Sticking with you through whatever you planned or set out to do
You were the only man she ever loved and knew

Gangsta bred
Galvanizing her soul
Addiction embarked on y'all paths
Then dysfunction led
Devouring everything you built
Submitting to the enemy wishes
Shattering our entire world to pieces

"Looking For You"

Im looking for you
The super hero I idolized growing up as a child under my roof

When his sole mission was to steal, kill and destroy
A life filled with loud noise
Playing with our souls as if they were toys

But sorrow said it was you
Pointing fingers whos to blame
This whole life cycle is a game
Fortitude, Mentally strong in order to regain
From all the shame and pain

Im still looking for you
In every man I befriend
Searching for that win even if I sin
But you compared to none of them
When my every choice was a continual rigged failed gamble spin

But I was looking for you
The one that sat me down as a child teaching me how to tie a shoe
Everything has been misconstrued
You left me alone to stand here and speak our truth
Honestly its tough because Im still needing and missing you
Neither one of us knew
What this traumatic dominoe effect would do
Or even who we would lose

I just pray to see you again and until then
I'll continue to search for that sign in this time
Looking for you
Just to let me know your doing fine
Proud of my growth and how Im openly letting my light shine
I sit and think about you daily reminiscing through these rhymes

Im looking for your humor
The laughs I found when I was sad
It could only be you dad
Ive matured and moved foward detaching from the mad
Holding on to all the past memories that we had
Of how we hit them streets like Bonnie and Clyde
Sticking by each other side
Damn I wish you were still alive
Ill continue to keep my focus and thrive
But I really miss you
And Im still looking for you

Dedicated to my late father Robert M. Mcghee

"Young Seva"

My last bae
And if I could do it all again
I would hold you so close to my heart throughout all of my days

Its so much that I wanna show you
Only me and God knows the extent of how bad I want to hold you
I dont know if I told you

I wish I could erase and take on all of your pain
Sometimes just the thought of you hurting will drive me insane
But just by me hearing your voice over the phone and seeing you smile in photos
momentarily some what eases my strain

I want you to please understand and know that even though Im away that my love
is still here and will always remain the same

We have better days coming ahead
So be strong and courageous and continue to always hold up your head

Your my last and final seed
My unique Columbian son with the heart shaped birthmark planted on the side
of your head

I admire your strengths continue to stay focused
And fed from the promises our almighty God has spoken
Trusting and believing that you are one of the chosen

"Runaway Child"

Carelessly running through time
Miles over miles
In search of missing pieces
To fill in the vacancies of empty hollow holes of incompleteness
In attempts to discover your true smiles

Abandoned and Scorned
Questions sent up to GOD like why was I even born
The absence of both biological parents have left you emotionally torn
Encumbering pain, Mentally abused
But no one can feel the agony inside those worn out shoes

Holes in both soles
Souls and soles
From running your life race
An undeveloped childhood that has been mis-placed
With chasing dysfunctional trauma
Thats been finishing in first place
Winning the defeating battle
Scoring a trophy that enemy adores
With no instilled artillery you stagger in perplexity
Ignoring the genuine love thats warm and welcoming
Opening up its doors

Obstructing barriers, Plague carriers
Invading your thought process, Creating a disheveled mess
Leading you deeper further out in the wilderness of desperation
Broken and lost
Not realizing that your losing and could soon pay the cost

While addiction is at its peak
Your mommy strength grows weak
Begging for you to please go home
To the home that is not your perceptible own

The extended love that I pray that you could see
Feeling and embracing the love of your sisters and brotherly
Love or what about G-O-D
The first love thats been showering you from up above
Protecting you from harm
In understanding of all your strong-arms

Behaviors and needs
Juvenile delinquency, Anger, Rage
As life read your storybook
With deductions of photograpic memorabilia pages

Its plain to see that your alone
I apologize multiple times over and over again for that sad song
That plays over and over in your mind

But runaway child
With afflictions of dereliction
If you wanna get ahead
Please stop running
Dont let those negative emotions consume you
And have you feeling mis-led

"Dynasty seed"

Precious cargo on board uncertain if its a boy or a girl
Gods blessing, Slightly stressing
My unique introduction to this world

Gotta tighten up and revise my focus
My innocent seed has been planted
A new edition to the family a devoted road Ive chosen

2023 a fresh year, A gracious start
My first Doctors visit I was administered revision after listening to your heart
Understanding that its my priority that me and my old behaviors depart

Precious cargo on board dont need no bumps or bruises
My addiction has been placed in the past
Dont wanna inflict any hurt so Im no longer use'n
So many questions why now? why me?
But ob-vi-ous-ly
There is something more that my Higher Power has planned for me to see
An alteration in my intended routes without any doubt
My life is not my own
Your precious valuable love and life inhabits my womb

Precious cargo on board with a more purposeful journey to explore
Conveying your freight, Accumulating your weight
Until I birth and unload
Your requisite beautiful blessing will then explode

Permeating my mold
The precious cargo thats hidden and suspensefully untold
Until its ran its allotted course to deliver and dock
And the incubation time has expired on its clock

"Inner Child"

My inner child seems to appear when Im stunned by fear and my circumstances
turn cold
Even though Im an adult shes still an infant incubated hidden deep inside my soul
When the weight of life pressure gets to heavy to bear
And my vigiliant eyes transform into blinded vision and Im no longer aware

When Im blindsided and hurt
When my love ones avert

The innocent child awakens with unrecognizable worth
Feeble searching for any consoling outlet to divert
Her speech had froze when uncomfortableness arose

When desecration debilitated our character
The spiritual nourishment of GOD was administered
Then exhilaration stimulated a fresh narrator

Shes just an ordinary ageless undeveloped child
And its been quite a while since Ive seen her smile
Camouflaged beneath my surface
Shes vicariously living through my skin for a purpose

"Since I Dont Know You Like That"

Since I dont know you like that
I do know your loyal and you have my first sons back
I know you stayed down with him through deep waters side by side riding them
rocky waves
Never abandoning him keeping his head afloat and not jumping off the boat

Since I dont know you like that
I know throughout his darkest days you conceived a child
A new extension to our family "Kali" a beautiful baby girl an innocent child
Thats keeping him focused working confined in the house not in the the streets
running wild
Shes currently shining the light in yall world
Giving my son a purpose in life
Praying you'll remain and continue forward an eventually become his wife

I know that your home stay clean and your not living trife
Keeping my son belly full resembling a part of my life

I know that your polished but still wont take no shit
And if you get pissed off you will be ready to hit

I also feel that you dont be on no other niggas dxck
Because I know that you know where you at is it

Since I know you like that
I just keep my mouth shut and sit
But just keep on thinking that I dont know shit

"Quest For The Woman In The Mirror"

My past identity has searched the world
In order to awake this lost broken little girl
And what it found was an extraordinary woman
Over the years of her mistakes and bad choices that was made
She was just a vunerable naive little girl in search for her pearls
Loose and wild

Throughout her journey shes had some twists and turns
Got tempted and manipulated, Swindled and burned
Lied, Mis-guided
And if it was trending she tried it
Partying
Drugs ignited her walk down many dark roads
Unhealthy relations
She began to engage in and more pressure was then exposed

Mother hood embarked
Placing her in another position filled with decisions desperate livin
Had to get it survival mode
So chasing currency is what she idolized
Now hustlin mode had paved her roads
And by any means necessary was the motto she chose

In the streets beatn her feet
Careless, Reckless
Toting a glock
waiting for anybody to try to check this
And in her mind she couldnt be stopped

Carrying packs, Imported
Elevated drug abuse, Mental health distorted
To many outsiders involved in her business, Extorted

Got completely knocked off of her feet
Landed a fifthteen year prison sentence
Her entire mission was aborted
She couldnt afford it

Not with those five innocent seeds
Her five children
The litter from her own breed

Not to mention the lost of her dad
So many memorable times
His sense of humor always and still makes her laugh
Although he was tied to her crime, Hes her light that still shines

But in her rehabilitation space
She finally looked in the mirror and got introduced to her true face
A woman thats been through the storm
One that has never lived a life of the average norm
Grateful to be reborn
And able to obtain all of the much needed tools she discovered
Throughout all of her storms

"Inherited Domestics"

Infatuated my lust and perception of you had steered me wrong
The glowing flame that once burned so bright in my soul no longer light up this happy home
It has dimmed its light
Multiple bruises from the fights night after night
There was numerous unsettled quiet hidden issues that became apparently loud over time
You were solely mine a masculine figure that appeared to be effectively fine

However your uncontainable behaviors screamed out a sound and smell of injurious abuse
It began to leak and reek our connection grew weak
You displayed a cold frozen heart that was love proof
No authentic love could break through
Your upbringing experiences in life had damaged you as a youth

As a child your father was present but he manufactured street addictions and physical abuse
He was loose and trauma was introduced
So you witnessed a grieving mother that fought relentlessly to rectify and maintain a family unit
Without a life or emotional manual
She went through life accepting being mishandled

Then their was you disrespectful and rude beneath the surface
That is what was embedded in you
No real love or respect for any woman that you would choose
Emulating your father shoes you will repeatedly lose

Inner and outer blues
Emotional and bodily blemishes

You would paint my body with color
Apologetically kiss me again just to pretend to be my lover
Expressing to me that this time there wont be another
But simultaneously your kisses, fists and anguish will smother
Me with suffocations of mental and physical abuse

I had to flee I had to break loose
Encouraging myself with the truth
There have to be brighter paths that we both can choose
Today Ive escaped and thats living proof
Inherited Domestics
Reach out for help there is better roads we can choose

"Rotation"

The recycled dysfunction repeating generation after generation
Im yearning to know the proper solution to heal this cycle confusion
And to defeat the noxious pollution
Of our upcoming seeds
That have multiple voids and vacancies yearning for their needs
Combating with lingering stains of over spilled trauma
From spectator views of the physical abuse beating and driven addictions in their
Momma
Engraved on the brain
Making it impossible to maintain
And live peacefully sane
And as the children grew into adulthood that broken inner child remained
incubated in their souls
Bereaving over what was deficient
Privy to the hidden events that have yet to be exposed
Searching for the answers of their youth hood that they barely can tolerate to
mention
The exposure to drugs has captured their attention
Now they are even more distant
Out of reach not wanting to be touched
Isolated in the cold, Running the streets
Not understanding that in sober reality their Mother heart really wanna love and
hold them so much
On the surface their disposition is hard and tough, Their scarred
Not easily to approach
This is a rehearsed, recycled story thats so continually rewrote

Poetically Me

Urban Lyrics

"What We Do"

We innovate, With passion we influence fashion
We debate when injustice separate
Our communities and culture
The unsettling racism afflicting upon us torture
Overstated prison sentences
Ongoing traps of recidivism

We do what we do
We make something out of nothing
Super naturally overcoming
Our obstacles and trauma of life
Breaking free from strongholds
Gods forgiving grace and mercy for several chances to get it right

Turbid and dirty we get it out the mud slimy and sticky
We brainstorm our lack putting our notions into motion
In hopes that God send his blessing from up above

We take risks with the willingness to lose to gain
Victoriously surpassing the presumed limits of our disadvantages
Setting new standards in society
Entering unfamiliar jurisdictions, The unknown, Doing what we do

We set newfangled trends
The greatest achievements through sport wins
We win
Defying the odds
Making the impossible, Possible
We ball, We fall

And with driven perseverance with bounce back up standing tall
Resilient were brilliant
With uprooted strengths from our ancestry shoes
We could never lose
Holding on to our powerful jewels

Consuming the proper knowledge and not living life as fools
We do what we do

"Sexual Orientation"

This is our day of sexual orientation
Come on get closer
Guiding me on to more stimulating destinations
The day we both unite, Igniting our entangled love actions
Mutually exposing our sexual preference information

Caress and explore my body its pure elation
While Im enjoying every bit of this encounter
The impact of your touches has took me on a heightened emotional flight
Depositing a variety of notions
Im moaning out loud, My bodies going wild
With no regrets of the cause or affects
Of these physical motions, Mixing up magical potent love potions

The combat is on
Were groovn and movn to the cadence of the music playing from this satisfying
love song
A battle I dont wish to lose
On the field I display an ordance of artillery
Im distributing, Its totally up for you to choose
Whisper in my ear and let me know what position you'll use

Were setting the rules as we go
You say turn around, Then up, Then down
Its on the flo
The more we tangle Im feeling your tool grow
Propelling me to mount up, No front
I gotta prolong this adventurous show

Begging you for more
Annihilation of one another as we venture off into more
Neither one of us are bothered with taking the time out to record or even view
the score
Ive given you permission to freely explore

"O" but wait a minute honey thats an explicit door that we both must ignore
We could never get bored

Understand my foreign language that Im speaking through these sounds
Im lovin your drop down
Now bring it back up to my face, Sharing the taste
With wet kisses as you ascend from the ground

Im bound
These feeling are analytically profound
Our combined interest and beliefs
Ive given you the title as chief
Taking charge of this sexual orientation

An imperative requisite lead
My open introduction
Thats satisfying my every sexual need

"The Art Of a Lier"

The entire time it wasnt really you
It was an imposter mis-leading me in directions that only your deceiving ways
would do
In intent to create false facades
Living separate lives with connections to multiple broads

The way you chose to fill your shoes
Placing me in a variety of positions to lose
Wasting my valuable precious time making me feel like a fool
Your a superficial ass fraud
Covering all of your tracks
Tied to numerous infidelity contacts
A lier with elaborate skills

And over the past years of these artificial thrills
I have never perceived this characteristic within you
Love with the premonition to kill
O yea I gotta bagg back

Lies on top of lies
Lying about lies
Now who the hell does that
Characterized trickery eyes with abilities to disguise
Yourself in that welcoming mask that had me hooked

But now just consider me as another piece of puxxy
And additive to your little black book
As you were maneuvering in secrecy
My intuition was telling me that you were cheating on me

At first my heart was not allowing me to believe my conviction
Until you started magically disappearing
M.I.A.
Missing

Then I bumped into one of your broads and your name was mentioned
She defined you to a 'T' even the tinyest description
Thats the main reason that I gathered us all here together to carry on this intervention
But you wanna continue to scheme and fib

The exact kind of scandalous factitious life that you choose to live
Im just so glad that I aint have your kids
We can detach and be through with this shxttttttt

"Jealous"

Im jealous incapable of stopping the way that I feel
They should prescribe a pill for the unwarranted emotions of the paranoid ill minded mates
Assuming that their lovers are being unfaithful out on undercover dates

In the others face and space
After they continuosly switch up schedules arriving home late
Planting thoughts of tangible bonding
Customary to what we were use to our connection finding
Because as of today your not responding

To me anymore behind our closed doors
And your eyes are no longer filled with the love that use to adore
Your wife
How you use to console me holding close and so tight
Assuring me that Im secure and will be foreverly be alright
With no alarm, No fright
I could feel it in my gut that something just aint right

Im jealous I dont know what has become of you
Youve been so distant and out of sight
And theres charges to our bank accounts that I dont recognize
Over the years I got use to being rewarded every night
You havent surprised me in a while
Ran off gone is the absence of my smile
I thought I was your wife
But now we barely communicate you walk around wearing a disguise
You have me confused I thought you were my prize

My intuition say be jealous
I understand its an ugly attribute but what the hell is
We doing anymore
Should I just walk around operating in mechanical mode and just ignore

Your newly revealed steps
The missing money from our bank accounts from the unannounced written checks
My rejections and neglect
Now you know I could be at your neck
But whats the use

Im jealous what the heck

You reek of a infidelity smell
One that is not of my own
Its a red button you pushing that can convey me to prison
And take me away from our use to be so happy home

Ima have to leave you alone
Because Im jealous

Phobia of Love

Ever since my previous love downfall Ive had an intense phobia of heights
And ever since youve entered my life landing your unique compassion
Im back in the proximity of the floating clouds in the sky now flying on your love flight
You buckled the seatbelt and told me that it was securely strapped so tight
And no matter how much I attempt to question and contend your actions you oppose and say our connection is worth all the fight

Its feeling like heaven when Im next to you
You stating that you want my love 365 days
24/7 calling me your Boo

Im afraid with conflicting thoughts and emotions
Repeatedly asking the question of how I became your chosen
Reluctantly, How do I respond
Weve already started to build and bond

Perplexed not knowing what to do
Flying blind uncertain of my destinastion with you

Whats foreseen in our future for the two
Only God knows
I wish that he would present us with at least one clue

Your love is
So welcoming, Delightful
But my past toxic failed relations cant help but resurface negative thought barriers
In attempts to sabotage our relationship cycle
Being so maliciously spiteful

Consol me, Show me
Let me know why I got presented this golden ticket to aboard this flight
For you to come close and get to know me

Your the pilot flying this plane
Question
Where are you taking me during our travel

Mutually receptive
We both are recognizing what we can bring to the table
Displaying our authentic values
Feeling so blessed to have you

Up floating so high above
The turbulence coming from your kisses and touches
Are shaking up my capacity for our love

The proposal words thats gliding my emotions, Frightened
Leaving me speechless, Conversation frozen

Asking to turn me into your Missus
Phobia of Love
What is this?

"Insignificant Others"

Insignificant others
And not your lovers
My sisters and brothers
Im speaking on those that love to hate
In attempts to rob you from your achievements and goals
While you trying to pave your success roads

They wanna eat off your plate
Relishing when you fail
Never congratulate unless its fake
There much lesser than great
Sitting on the sideline stuck, Idle, Watching
Spectators of their own life race
But still have the time to check your place
In your life race

Social media stalkers, Patroling, Trolling
Merchandise tagging, Placing lables
PH.D Doctor diagnosing
Preschooled with your jewels, They fools
But let them tell it they know everybody news
CNN, HLN
The only 9 to 5 they ever worked is bumping their gums
Shooting from the hip, Burning rubber on them lips

UPS drivers
Making sure the gossip is twisted, Safety delivered
Mess on Mess
Derived from their deficiency and stress
Or resistance in their walk

So they continually feed off of negativity and stir up talk
About this n that, Whos wack, And got sent back
In the back with them, Consumed with lack
Instead of looking in the mirror self-evaluating their tracks
Now whats up with that

Get acquainted with your true reflection
But I understand thats what your fearing
Diversion steering
Because they cant face
Face to face

Thats why they stagger and stumble
And then insist to mumble
Asking questions like why they stuck in the same place
Broke down on the side of moving traffic

Stagnant not able to reach
Or abide by what is preached
Cant move ahead, Mis-led
Not moving forward
Walking backwards in life instead

Insignificant others

"Creep"

So I creep
Sleeping around on the down low
With the other my undercover lover
That satisfy my vacant needs
And with his occupancy I try to restrain myself from the actions of infidelity

But this creeping continues to get the best of me
He appeases my hunger
Our sexual orientation is thunder
Lightning striking all the right spots
Hes hot
Electrifying sensations, Elation

Perpetual motions I think I got it bad
Im beginning to never want him to stop its sad
So I creep

We both have to stay on alert keeping a close eye at the clock
Because my husband of ten years is expecting me back home at around 2 o'clock
Just alone the others presence makes me moan
And that keep leaving my husband at home alone persistently calling my phone
Compelling me to fabricate this pile of excuses
Whats the use of me taking my vows
If the plan for our future was for me to rearrange our smiles
We done walk through so many miles

Together and now Im covering up my true disruptive behaviors
Of why Im on the outside of the relationship being the loosest exchanging sexual favors
Piloted by my warranted euphoric emotional thrills
Initiating my convulsions and chills
So I creep, So we chill

Frequently texting your line like where can we meet
Sneaking and geeking wearing a disguise
Im discreet
Met you at the room on the other side of town you put it down and we both fell asleep

Slipping I didnt awake until the next morning it was about a quarter too three
And my husband had been blowing my phone up wondering where I could be
trying to contact me

Disheveled I scuffled out the room jumping into my vehicle turning the key
But as I attempted to back out the parking lot spot my husband appeared blocking
me in as his astonished eyes were set directly on me
Stating please dont let this be true what I see
Is this what you truly want
Exposed it was out in the open
This not what I was hoping
To happen and he was scoping me up and down with looks to kill
Then he asked again is this the road you have chosen

Disloyal disposing all the progress we sustained
Am I insane
Is this the lane that I have honestly chosen
I was stunned I couldnt even speak
But the aroma of the creep just wouldnt let me decide in peace

It had started talking
My legs took off on their own and started walking
Back towards the room
Taking them steps back from me jumping the broom
In love and making vows with my groom
My mouth spoke and the verbage on my tongue had sung
I apolojize and tears began
To run from my eyes
So please just let me be
Because I just want to creep
So I creep

"Impostors"

Impostors never tapping into their authentic identity
They rather follow the trending herd
For what its worth telephoning passing around the gossip that is heard
Emulators, Violators, Haters not recognizing the substantial greater
Exposing facades on social media sites
Factitious views of the unreal happiness in their lives
Whats right, Whats life the reception of likes
Or the boosted self-esteem vibes feeling the vacant voids in their lives
Human validation unfortunately ignites some being lights
A complex way to live its an emotional rollercoaster flight
Combating against self-confidence is such a harsh injurious way too live life
As an impostor

"Imposter

"The Gamble"

With exposed access to the streets I took off running head first
I slid and fell getting stuck in between the enemy cracks of the asphalt
I couldnt point fingers at anyone or anything else
To justify my actions solely responsible
In total acceptance it was all my fault

The fast life was cold
And over time engaging in the activities put miles on your body
At young age it presented you as old
Placing a whipping internally and externally to your created mold

But the excitement had me addicted
In search for that mighty dollar
Prowling in the late night after hours
Corruption embarked
Then aching consequences was afflicted

Bonnie and Clyde unhealthy relationships
Thugg'n
Soliciting ourselves and drugs for the devil we were the plug in our hood

Running the streets day and night with lives built around hustl'n
For that quick come up
Up to no good with misconstrued priorities
Our direction for life was misunderstood

Living life risky without any rules
The streets were ruthless so we stayed with protection toting tools

The Gamble

Ride or die chick
Realizing today that that cliche had to be set in stone for immature fools
That lacks the knowledge of their true worth
The unfamiliar power thats held within
The unknown abilities needing to be extracted
Instead of allowing the lifestyle to keep you distracted

Because their are many of us that rode and got robbed of our precious jewels
Stagnant, Lost stuck in the game
Depreciating our temple for that renown hood fame
Complacent on them restless streets
Consumed by the noxious heat

And its so unfortunate for the lost ones that jumped onto those undefeated rocks
of the asphalt
Bumpy gravel, Hurdled streets
Entering into this deadly race to compete
Only to get rewarded with utter defeat

Now 6 ft. deep
Underneath the dirt they sleep
An early death's retirement is what they greet
A time clocked stopped devouring undeveloped, mis-guided lives to soon
A mankind expired
Something the enemy admires

While street recognition and wealth is what was taught and so enticingly aspired
Now they gone to soon
With faded memories appearing in loom
Anyone attempting to gamble and battle these streets are destined to be doomed

"Relational Meet"

Once I was shot by Cupids arrow I fell in love with a distasteful youth
Street proof, Gangsta deuce
Displaying indisposable truths
Living life as a man, Fitting teenager pants, Adolescent stance
With defective qualities of all the wrong things, Crime scenes
Imitating the exact attributed reflections of the superhero men that I idolized in my upbringing
Perplexed about what my vision was seeing
In my distorted reality he was the man of my dreams
We had formed teams
Embarking on many indescribable schemes
In the preliminary I was the visionary
Painting our life imprints on canvas towards luxurious themes
Allowing you to plant our innocent seeds
Which prompted me to perform my supernatural motherly deeds
And as I conceived
Inherited addiction arose, My love had froze
I was uneducated broke the vows and had to leave
So a single mother was the road I chose
As the dysfunction fully awakened, It put a halt to what I perceived we were making
I placed connections in more wholesome destinations
Resetting and embarking on my own journey
Independately, Single dressed, The grass was greener
It was fitting me the best
I departed
Discoveries through my failures made me smarter
Wisdom was released when life experienced test were breached
The weight was lifted, My disposition shifted
You deprived me from certain portions of my maturity
Spreading my wings and flying away is what cured me
But my inner chid still lives shes not deceased
My Higher Power unsealed my sight and hearing, Im no longer blind
Attentive to the living word thats preached
And in all honesty and belief the fruit we produced was worth the meet
And the skills Ive obtained were my most valuable learned needs
This is just one version of my life lesson experienced relational meet

"Margin"

I need margin come on gimme my space
To many haters on watch, Surveillance
Facades of false interest concerns, Noisey
All up in my face
Put some space between yo words
Cause you got to much to say, Social media, Clockn my page
Knowing my every move day after day
Gimmie margin, Im comin in
To win, my creative skills go pave the way
Im that star in the night
That still shining with an illuminating mindset
Provinding light, Thats here to stay
With another shot, Blessed every 24 hours presents a new day

I need margin gimmie my space
You come to close I gotta spray, Not the type to play
So if I dont know you stay the fxxk out my way

I keep a small circle inside a circle
So dont introduce yourself, No need to say hey
The less I know the less confusion
Keeping that negativity off of my plate
Pushing it outta my way

I need space
Dont need no loud noise where I lay
My home is where I take the time to meditate, Collect my thoughts
Figuring out my next play

I need margin from those men
That keep approaching me presenting themselves as if we were friends
Just to tap on my laptop, Hit, Delete
And then send me on my way spreading me thin
Vigilant
I see them coming thats how I remain ahead
And they cant grab that chance to begin

Margin, All Im saying is gimmie my space if you can relate

"F.W.T.B."

Im not about to stress over no man but nevertheless
You fucking with the best
So there is no need to contest
My broken cold heart pieces been numb
Ive experienced taking the heat up under the gun
So in contentment I will confidently stand strong
Never stunned or foolish sprung

Ten years down it was rough but I remain intact
My faith is what fortified me it stayed strapped across my back
Very candid so we go cut through all the slack
Infidelity no
I just dont tolerate any of that

Im not your average woman so dont consider me as less
Im just being honest I say you fucking with the best
Not your usual chick so dont compare me to the rest

Death before Dishonor
Lets resurface Fredo Corleone
Thats when the ultimate disloyalty had hit so close to home
Placing business before loyalty that type of shit will always lea you wrong
It had him knocked off blindsided on the boat right after Michael Corleone had
accepted him back into his family home

Im Gansta bred, Street game fed
So I dont understand why these artificial unstable creatures keep trying to test
me planting bullshit in my head

Misled these men are sick
Terminal they think with their dicks
And Im the designated physician delivering the news of how long they have to live
So quit coming at me sideways feeding me the bullshit

I get straight to it
G.A.M.E. Getting At My Enemies
Renown hood fame

And if its a formulated idea Ima do it
My business is straight up %100 fluid
Like the ocean and my every deposited lucrative notions that I attempt to put
into motion

Innovator, Fuck a hater, Hood relator
Done mastered the game
Took off gone Ill catch up with you later

Never accustomed to the shredded beef
Im vegan I love to keep my digestive system clean
Settled in peace
No beef, No meat
Sometimes I can feel a little pescatarian
A fish that has matured and grew to big for this tank
Extract me out of this small aquarium

Throw me in the water with the sharks
Im ready they pose no alarm
Im fear resistant let me get acquainted and speak and see how they think boldly
ascertain Im not worried about the harm
But you keep trying to kiss me then diss me
All you niggas is some sissies

No male will penetrate me
Im on new avenues with lesser issues because Im at my best
And Im not about no stress
Thats not apart of my future plans you fucking with the best
I could never lose
Never meddling or settling with a fool

I have no time today my time is valuable Im cool
Again you fucking with the best I have discovered my jewels
So what you want to do
Im strangely unique surpassing the average Im new

So dont compare me to the rest
One last time so you can fully understand that you fucking with the best
So please quit insulting me trying to put me to the test

"That's Why They Call Me Bitch"

Thats why they call me bitch
But they dont understand that I carry a traumatizing past from my childhood
that sticks
When my temple was solicited for drugs so my parents could get their fix
My purest innocence was stolen
My adolescent body parts were swollen

There was no where I could turn to
No authorities patrolling
So I grew to to be a connoisseur to this life
I wasnt made to fit the position as any man wife

Thats why they call me bitch
And thats the exact description that I like because it fits
I know it aint right
But I lived this way my entire life
Numerous johns
Risky encounters encompassing me in harm
Never alarmed

Because it was an accustomed routine
I had a few dreams
Of wishing to relinquish all of these damaging engrained things
But my inherited behavior and nature of my character continued to mislead me
making me waver

So thats why they call me bitch
And now its not only my parents but its me thats searching for that fix
Hitting licks
Taking multiple hits
Affliction had mentally stripped
Me down consumed with the dysfunction in total despair
This shit wasnt fair
Impaired

As I stare down the long road Ive traveled
So how dare
You judge me and call me a bitch
Im just that chick
That was inbred to hit these licks from tricks
Thats why they call me bitch

"Immunity"

All my life I never consider circumstances as a fight
My struggle came easy
Now does that mean that Im immune to strife

My heart turned cold
Pressure wont dampen my mold
Ive completely accepted that when we grow old our lives will then began to fold

Death lurks in the loom
Insanely immune
Agony grooms my day as I continue to pray
I just keep it pushing allowing perseverance and resiliency to pave my way

Penetrating trauma doesnt phase me
I consume smoke daily its my inherited normalcy
Theres not to much that Ive noticed that will bother me
Fear resistance, Invulnerable disposition
Exposure you wont miss it, And if you diss it
Ima kiss it open and available for war
Put you to sleep in a blink of the eye
Quick making them snore

Give me more
My life is a movie so Im never bored
Enter at your own risk
Im immune to this shit but whos keeping score
Immunity

Left Overs

Scraps, You may of had him first
But he ran to me to get nursed

Resuscitated back to life
Hold up Wait a minute
Dont get it misconstrued I could never be his wife
Im just here to console and give advice
Sending him back home to your table after I keep him for a couple of nights

Scattered scraps, Im all over the map
So anything I eat is freshly picked no need to bother me with all that
More over, Left over set out to spoil
I slaughter meat daily just to season
Turn up the heat and broil
Bak'n niggas, Shak'n niggas
No brain because Im familiar with the food chain
Im kinda pesky
Plant-based & seafood mainly vegetarian lane

Scraps, You can have em I surpassed them all
He rep'n my name
I ate off him for a while
I say Im send'n him back but you still insist to wanna brawl

Late night after hours solo no date I pull up for take out
Couldnt eat it all I had to leave some on my plate
Thats the generosity my Higher Power installed

Make me over, To the beholder
My scraps, Left overs
The collected remnants of my explosive past
Salvaged, put back together
A master piece thats rebuilt to last

Never greedy, Feed'n the needy
I eat less I perfer my tank on E
Glut-to-ny to nothing but G.O.D.

His nutritional bread is my main source that F.E.E.D.S. me
The best his prophetic word I confess

Buffet Holy spirit filled to the max
Individuals stacked back to back
Mess'n over his food leaving tampered tracks
Left over impacted scraps
Now how you feel about that?

"What Yo DNA hit Fo"

The paparazzi clock'n like we models in a show
Ugly people dont be petty
Im camera ready stay rock'n steady
What that DNA hit fo

Im in the sto then right back out the do
Because strange eyes are surveillance watching
Stopping traffic like wo
What that DNA hit fo

Im thanking God for my genes
My reflection in the mirror stating
I cant complain if you could see what I mean
My beauty runs deep
Interior and exterior
From my head to my feet

Elegantly born
I give the credit to my parents for their perfect collaboration when I was formed
What yo DNA hit fo

Bribery schemes
I got niggas in my DM dropp'n semen
Try'n to impregnate me
Cash and gifts for my genes
Beauty slay'n I aint play'n
Ugliest the least
Ima ostracize the beast
Send the animal off to exile isolated
To roam and growl

Now what yo DNA hit fo
Because my bloodline runs deep
From my children to their children
And any of the rest of my lineage that you meet

My sister look good
My brothers masculine beauty is understood
My nieces my nephews amplified beauty speaks
"You good"

Blessed with the best
Leverage over all the rest
And if you ugly then Im truthfully sorry that your simmering in that mess

Im not arrogant or conceited
But my confidence is most definitely needed

What yo DNA hit fo
My ancestry tree is never weak
With no stress the roots are developed strong
Unfortunate individuals stay angry always ready to brawl
They be wrong

I carry no beef on my chest
You take the challenge and put it to the test
My DNA is A-1 potent
And Ima tell you once again that Ive been blessed with the best

What that DNA hit fo

"What You On"

(verse)
You say Im burning
You steady yearning for me calling my phone
If Im infected then neglect it
Quit trying to get me to bone
What you on

Chorus)
What you want, what you on
Aint got no time to waste
Lets keep it one-hundred on the surface
Baby Ima keep it real and put it all up in yo face
So lets not put on fronts
I just wanna relax and chill while we puffing on these blunts
You knew from the jump off that I was a skunk
(verse)
Raw and promiscuous
You done dodged a bullet if you not feeling this
Trashy nasty if yo pockets on full you could have me
You not passing me

I could be pesky and sexy
And if you laying it right I could bring my bestie

Chorus)
(verse)
Lets get it started Im retarded
I led you on left you alone
A realist cause Im wrong
I dont belong
Im deceiving I'll just keep stringing you along

I like to spread my wings prevelent prone
Confusing myself about what I be on
But its on
What you on

"I Just Wanna Dance"

Exiting work on a Friday night I gotta keep it moving
Gotta groove to this beat
Spotted a club around the corner
With no concerns I entered not worrying about who I bump into on the dance
floor
I can careless who I meet

I just wanna dance all night long
Moving my body parts working up a sweat
Attracting heat with my arms placed around someones neck
And as I begin to sweat everything is disheveled
My appearance is no longer neat
The expression on my face welcomely greets

Men are making their way to the dance floor stalking
Jealous women are talking
As I get lost in my songs
I could dance all night long
The way they staring and pointing fingers you would of thought I was doing
something wrong

You gotta understand these feeling
Similar to Marvin Gaye emotions when he was singing sexual healing
The melodies flow through my soul
This type of mood could never grow old

Accelerating my movements to want to climb these walls and dance on the ceiling

O what a beautiful feeling
When you dealing with the cadence of the drums
With out a doubt it will have you rhythm sprung

Incited weekend energy
Getting loose having fun
And anything goes under this disco ball sun
Sexy, Soothing
On the dance floor grooving

Releasing the tension from a full weeks work on a Friday night
And everything is quite alright

Im trying to contain myself while Im twerking
The more I lose myself this skirt Im wearing is just not working
Afraid of indecent exposure
For letting my hair down for the weekend
On a partying disclosure

I just wish to unwind to some hits, Wind these hips
Letting the rhythm set me free and direct my motions
Prompting me to dance and provide me that fix
All night long the DJ is jamming
And the club that I chose is lit

I just wanna dance

"Complete Forgiveness"

Forgiveness is one of the fruits of the spirit thats embedded in my heart
So that had compelled you to cheat right from the very start

Never having intentions on settling down
You were spreading yourself thin all around this small town

I knew you would never confess
Because deceiving and lying is always what you have done the best

Putting all of your lovers to the test
Suffocating us with heartache until we take that last breath

Id advise you to do some house cleaning because your a filthy mess
I know karma is a bxtch and the time will come for you to be checked
Im sweet like candy but Im not weak
And with this continual acceptance of your disloyalty
My forgiveness is now obsolete

Replaced with someone of greater substance
You cant compete
Now dont appear dumbfounded you the one that decided to cheat
Understand thats its all over with us my heart is complete
Because as of now my forgiveness is obsolete

"Voices"

There are voices crying out loud screaming for help in the wilderness
In need of spiritual healing Im uncertain if anyone else even notice or are they
hearing them
They are lost and broken draped in total despair
Thirsty spiritually starving in famine visually impaired
Chewed up and swallowed by the noxious cracks of the asphalt
After relentlessly roaming the undefeated streets
Blind tunnel vision in survival mode they could never compete

Devoured by the trauma in life they simmered in their bottomless pits of defeat
Mis-led by lack
Neglected in lax they would impulsively react
Wearing careless unnecessary consequences across their backs
Immune to daily afflictions
Their paradise was the hood that they live in
Tragedy, Poverty, Hustling, Guns, Death
Fatherless figures oppressed
Driven by currency as the enemy put them to its test

In their minds streetlife is the only life I know mentality dressed
Our young minorities are now the soldiers on the front lines making ruckus
Enticingly introduced to straps they're lost their focus
Juvenile bred hitman so the stiff felonies wont stand a chance
How can we reach and assist them to cope with their voids
Without any possibilities of hope how could we approach
The lost and broken toys

Thats in the wilderness making all that noise
How can we manage their self-sabotaging outlets of addictions
Whats healing and fixing
The abusing distributing or using

Premeditated death dates
Suicidal temptations another form of escape
The mind is a battlefield and its hard to find peace in the midst of confusion when
life on life terms get real
So their reality is only an illusion in the midst of their confusion

I hear voices crying out loud in the wilderness
And I pray that someone reach them in enough time to heal them
Before this lurking evil kill or steal them
Lets be the beacon that guides them toward the light
Exposing them to a more significant purpose
Oppose to living life so reckless and worthless
Expressing to them that all things are possible with a reach
You can find your significance by defying the odds if you just stop and listen to
the words that the redeemer speaks

A change will come
Even with gradual progression we all will eventually overcome and make it to
our real paradise up in heaven

Voices

"I Look To Fine For You To Waste Any More Of My Valuable Peace And Time"

I had the nightmare of the worst date
Letting my heart guide my steps
Letting my love serenade
He had a dual diagnosis of love and hate
With continual transformations of the infidelity stage
My saint turned sinner
Just when I was convinced that I had fell in love with a winner

Because at our fancy restaurant dinner
He was confronted by a young tender
A promiscuous ratchet chick that exposed all his hidden truths
Showing me the recorded footage on her I-phone
When they were sex'n in my home under our roof
It was clearly my bedroom there could be no counter dispute
My heart was broken and hurt
As the blood gushed out rapid spurts
My temper arose
My stomach was nauseous I could have puked
It was the blindsided realization of the honest truth
Now what was I suppose to do

Invested so many relentless years adhering loyal to you
Now what avenue should I choose
Weighing my options
You the one thats gonna lose
Man this is some very disturbing news

"I Look To Fine For You To Waste"

I needed a moment to think
My emotions and thoughts were conflicting
Im confused
Hold up now this what we go do

Listen you lousy ass nigga you could pack all yo shit up
Honey hes moving with
Ive came to far out of my darkness
And today I consider myself a star that shines so heavenly bright
Illuminating a broad scope of light
Ive carried unfathomable weight inside these shoes
I have no visions or space for distractions
So I could never lose

Hes been a waste of my precious time
Hes compliments you best as a partner
Your photo shots are magnificently fine
You can have him girl
I look to fine
To waste another moment of my valuable peace and time

Two Different Roads

His masculine exterior was superior
Heavenly formed
Not of any other norm
But his interior was like crossing the path of a black cat
Several steps that you would rather retract, Take them back

Cursed with rehearsed beautiful flourishing lies
And when I gazed into his eyes
He would sweep me off of my feet
Taking me utterly by surprise

Not realizing that it was all a disguise
Every notion he put in motion I would gladly oblige

Conversation was thick
Ill, Sick wit it, He was sick
And with just one touch I was whipped
Infected wit it
A contagious bug
This man was similar to a drug
Like one of cupid shots of love
I needed debugged

Yes he was a thug
Gangsta bred
Ran them streets day and night soliciting drugs
Dont get it twisted
Im not stating that Im above a thug

Because thats a familiar reflected journey that I once dug
So I could never judge

Disruption would always follow him
Corruption bad luck
Close to death situations persistently tried to devour him
And as we got closer acquainted he effectively dug my heart out of my chest
Throwing it out the window onto the lawn

Using me as a part of his success
One of his beneficial pawns
Doing only what he know how to do best

Deceiving lying and cheating
For years I stayed down loyal believing
In us and what I thought we had
Building that solid foundation
Tight net family connected relations
Conceiving your children yes he was a dad

And for the majority of the time we had a blast
But it was two different mindsets
Driving towards separate destinations
With separated diverse revelations
Our love would never last

He started sampling his own product
Wearing that addiction mask
Steady needing a fixing
Turning up all day, Forehead glistening
He started being M.I.A.
Missing

"Two Different Roads"

Exiting left driving down all the desolated dark roads
Where the walking dead reside without any planned goals
Only stagnant lifestyles sitting on ice
With deteriorating frozen mentals
Projecting negative advice

Two different roads
And after following you so far I had to turn around
To retrieve my crown
Especially when we entered the city of clowns
I had to mature, Polish up
I had descened, I was lowered down

There was no more time to waste in life playing around
Noticing the light I went back and made that right
Turned my wrongs to rights
Revisions of new sight, You got that right

20/20 vision, Infra red I can see through the night
No more backwards livin

Today Im navigating through a more positive slower traffic
Solo, Me and you as one no more thats a no no

A smoother route without a doubt
Detached from all the manipulation, Im bail'n
Extreme excell'n
Break'n free from them binding chains

Now Im sweet sail'n down more heavenly roads
So grateful to have that chance to rearrange and turn around with change
We on two different roads and as of today Im okay with that

"Love Wont Let Me Love"

Love wont knock at my door not even on a sunny day
I patiently await staring out of the window
Listening to the children echos from their summer play

Love wont sing me no love songs
The cadence is off its all wrong
unable to catch the flow or beat of any significant other that I encounter
Its obsolete

Love wont let me love
It just wont do me right
It has left me alone shivering for so many cold dark nights
Vulnerable, filled with over spilling fright
Stunning my emotions
Traumatizing me for life

Love have never accessed an open easy door
Im relentlessly twisting and turning door knobs
Submissive, yearning for more
With anticipation of that pleasant door that I can adore
The one I can walk through for life
Compatible and bright
Not obscure
One that Im able to walk through turn around and lock it feel'n safe and secure
Love wont let me love

"How Am I Suppose To Love Again"

We displayed smiles, Tied lifetime vows
How am I suppose to love again
When my soul is still carrying around all these empty holes in them
At a certain point of time we both conceived thoughts of being lifetime friends
Ive always stood right by your side ten toes down even when my broken heart
had to mend

MARY J BLIGE stay down
As your disloyal tail ran so freely around this town
I stayed down through whatever I had your back
I'd hit them tracks
And when I had to I'd tote the strap
Without any questions I will gladly oblige and do just that I loved you only

TONI BRAXTON how many ways
I had insanely committed to be your personal slave
It was suppose to be us side by side throughout all of our days
Let me count the ways
Because I carried the majority of the weight
Placing no one above you
When your currency came in late

My supernatural love is what kept us during those dates
In addition to the provided food that I placed on our plates
I conceived all your children
Upfront and honest with you always letting you know exactly what I was doing
You knew of my every movements
Never missing a beat
And as our romantic melody played in my mind we were grooving
But you were still unsatisfied on the outside lusting and compelled to cheat
Intuitively I knew what you were doing

RAY J if I had one wish
I would wish I hadnt took that chance
Allowing you up in my space filling that position to be my man
Rearranging my steps wishing to recast my past times
Maybe then I wouldnt be sitting here in my feeling writing down these ill rhymes
How can I love again

With the combined companionship of two souls again
How can I fill these voided vacant holes within
After I have given you the best of me
Crossing every ocean and the multitude of seas
While the incomplete love you was given was only what my naive perceived eyes
could see

I just want relations to let me be
No restraints, no expectations or any warranted unexpected hurt
No excuses no complaints!!!
Just me alone loving me flying free doing me

"I m In Love Again"

Im in love again
And all those vacant holes that was held within
Are filled with a special kind of occupancy
An unique love thats worth my time
A mature intimate connection

One that alleviates the weight
Dont violate
The head of the household take charge type of man that dont mind putting food
on the dinner table
He perfer me to eat off his plate
Never late hes always on time
Street life unaffiliated
With a legitimate for sure grind
And he dont carry any expectations
WALE on chill
I can get fully rested

STACY LATTISAW we the perfect combination
I couldnt ask for anyone better
Our feeling and souls collide perfectly meshed together
No on can do me better
Collectively combined as one we can weather any weather
The stormier the better
Because thats when the strategic robust built foundation is tested
Unable to be moved is confirmation that the good Lord has blessed it

For every rhyme and reason
Will stand together as that unbreakable force remaing firm through any hurricane
season
I was free flying lonely alone
With no restraints

Until this fresh love blew in blowing against the wind
With no insecurities we both trust one another when were apart flying so free
And when its time for us to find our way back home where we belong in each
others arms is exactly where we will be

Im no longer toting the strap in the streets hitting them tracks
Imperfections in all we remain loyal to one another
We stay down no matter the issue we have each others back

Im in love again and it genuine
A soldier with no excuses or complaints
This love done hit a home run
Invested we both are seriously committed not just doing this shxt for fun

Im IN LOVE AGAIN

"A Love Thats Worth My Time"

A love thats worth my time is when two souls collide and combine
Master minding grinds
But the grind is not what the Love defines
We can mentally connect without our relationship being based around a check
Now dont get it twisted his masculine ambition will legitimately work to protect
Providing taking care of home
No infidelity so he never roam
Staying down loyal reciprocated respect

A thug Love thats worth my time isnt afraid to humanize his voice
Admitting his fears and hurt,Unveiling his tears, open, honest
Exposing everything when hes at his worst
Revealing the naked heart
Vulnerable right at the initial start
Submissive, self-disciplined and sacrificial
But still wearing the title of the head of the household leading authority official

A thug that can express his most inner emotions in depth
Inner and outer beauty but can still strap up and transform and get ugly when hes put to the test
Inherited streets
But still spiritual we can pray together dropping down to our knees
Creating miracles, Available for change
Letting the living word rewrite our stories
Gods light, Rearrange
Aspiring towards new beginning, Lesser sinning, Only winning

A Love thats worth my time will withhold no fears
Envisions of eternity, Time elapsing, Years
Receptive to a thug love being mine.
Just could be that love thats worth my time

"Make Me Feel"

Make me feel like a drug that hits the blood
Elevating my heartbeat to more rapid thuds
Make me fall in love Im willing to sample and gamble a piece of your love
With high hopes to win slot machine spin
My entire world around like a strenuous whirlwind

Or like the young carefree children at the park playing on the merry go round
Spin me around and around until Im dizzy
Inebriated %100 proof love
Cupid struck floating on the clouds above
All smiles no frowns making me feel good

Lets be silly and laugh through life like we are at the dentist inhaling the gas mask
Or the jocuse spirit filled clowns
Chauffeur me through this town exposing me to greenery scenery
Securing any other accessible open doors
Protection locking me in so that surely I know that Im yours

Liberate my soul amplify my spirit
So my self-esteem will be reassured daily and forevermore tenaciously grip it
With a noise sounding off an alarm so loud that the entire planet will hear it
Make me feel good not allowing me to be a disheveled mess
Depressed be my soldier in armor
My melatonin assisting me to receive my proper rest
Overall peace nothing less

Withstanding all life issues Ill continue to boldly walk through this journey as
my best
Make me feel good a true partner that will reciprocate my love mentally grasp it
and have it understood

Keeping me lifted just love me make me feel good

"Snapping Season"

Snapping season Im praying and slaying rhythms for no apparent rhyme or reason
Rapid breathing done caught a victim in my trap and now they believing
Im now the one they seeing
Seething hot got to make it to the top and secure my spot
Before its to late because my time is receding

Although Im in full understanding that it is never to late to pursue my dreams as
long as my heart is still beating
Confident standing on faith I will always believe in
The almighty source that will usually direct or change my course
In his time when ever he decides to snap the season

Poetically aggressive with a heart full of love so my every encounter vision is
blurred due to this mysterious beacon of light that Im beaming

Diverse versatile manic sporadic formulated genes from my genealogy tree
through the DNA that my parents were breeding

It snapping season
Focused arose now chosen to resuscitate and breathe life into the broken lost
souls that the enemy is leading
Resilient undefeated posing no harm
Setting off elevation alarms with triumphant charms

Exuding that if you put your mental to it it can be done
Victim to victor, Testimonial child is what this snapping season has sprung
Its snapping season

"Get Yo Life"

Get yo life
Instead of being out here living so trife
Pointing the finger at everyone else to justify
Your feeble actions
Fulfillment of enjoyment your subtracting
Missing out on the true beauty of this secular land that we are entrapped in

What does your purpose mean
Man made deprived conditions still let your liberty ring
Recalibration of a second chance in life just makes me wanna sing
Two lives in one my Higher Power is dominion over everything

Protection keeping us in the palm of his hands
Guidance he left his footprints in the sand
So get yo life he holds the power he is the man
Supernaturally it is administered to us so take your stand
And get Yo life

"Mixed Emotions"

With a dual diagnosis of love and hate
You kept me perplexed I couldnt relate
I was infatuated by what you exhibit
Before I could get intimate with your mental or inner spirit

You resembled day and night
You didn't want to reciprocate my love something about you just aint right
You would tell me that you love me but then blemish my soul and pursue a fight
Serving me a daily dosage of your evil spite
Despite of my overwhelming comforting love that persisted on wrapping you up
to exude out all of those vicious confused emotional cycles of hate and love

My soul is beat down its purple
The mixture of your love and hate elements are ingredients for a disaster
Your specific type of love language that incites combustible tempers now is that
the type of affection that your after
Your inner soul crys for help but your full of laughter
Such a bizarre individual and loving you makes two
So our relationship with all these roller coaster rides of mixed emotions are now
obsolete it dont even matter

Carry on in laughter
Because as of today Ive broke free from the bondage of that crippling master

Mixed Emotions

"Infidelity"

If I tell you I love you will you be here to stay
Those were the very words that paved the way to my soul
Brightening up my days
You promised me that you would hold my heart close to yours and get lost in this time and never go astray
Keeping it protected never neglect it

But now we fussing and fighting and those very words no longer govern my heart
Your actions are tearing our once so happy home apart
Disloyal inconsistency your in the players field running plays with other women
The owner of a football team cheating leaving me home alone letting my mental roam
That shit is getting old your to grown your wrong
Im sweet but you have turned me sour
Creeping around the town especially during the late night hours

Having the audacity to come in late and tuck me in
Kissing my forehead telling me you love me whispering the words goodnight and you would place no one above me

Not realizing that your making it home the same time that the sun is halfway up gleaming shining its florescence light
Honestly Im tired of the fights
So Ima lay here on my side of the bed squeezing my ass cheeks tight
Until you get this shit right or before I pack my bags and flee some where far away out of reach and out of sight

My love and time is of the essence
You need to quickly generate a resolution and stop testing me
Infidelity will not keep stressing me or neither be the death of me
Why do your love has to be a battle that wrestles me
Im in need of reciprocity
A peaceful authentic love thats blesses me

So infidelity please stop testing me
Because Ive given you the best of me

"Things We Just Dont Seem To Understand"

Things we just dont seem to understand is that we were all created to perform in love as one on one accord similar to the making of the band

Every nationality and religion standing together in unity hand to hand
But theres an evil disrupting fan blowing corruption polluting our terrain in attempts to devour our God given land
We have the insanity of unfortunate suicide a thing we just dont seem to understand
Life gets impossible for some to mentally maintain
But when heaven open up its flood gates and send its rain
Drinking from its fountain will assist us to refrain
From the ill will and penetration from these unusual unexpected circumstances that insist on permeating our domain

Remember our sovereign orchestrater remains
Dominion over all
The plans that he had for us were not intended for the symphony to fall
But with love and understanding we can regain control over the plagues and form a more harmonious musical
United diversity in a more robust position standing tall
Effectively sufficient with love towards all
Even when the unexpected occur
The things we cant explain
The things we just dont seem to understand
The casualties of revelations the things that contradicts the master perfect plan
The things we just dont seem to understand